Michigan

BY AMY VAN ZEE

Published by The Child's World®
1980 Lookout Drive • Mankato, MN 56003-1705
800-599-READ • www.childsworld.com

ACKNOWLEDGMENTS
The Child's World®: Mary Berendes, Publishing Director
The Design Lab: Design and production
Red Line Editorial: Editorial direction

PHOTO CREDITS: Larry Ebbs/iStockphoto, cover, 1, 3; Matt Kania/Map
Hero, Inc., 4, 5; Gary Blakeley/iStockphoto, 7; Curt Pickens/iStockphoto,
9; iStockphoto, 10, 13; WDG Photo/Shutterstock Images, 11; North Wind
Picture Archives/Photolibrary, 15; Douglas Allen/iStockphoto, 17; AP Images,
19; Thomas Barrat/Shutterstock Images, 21; One Mile Up, 22; Quarter-dollar
coin image from the United States Mint, 22

LIBRARY OF CONGRESS CATALOGING-IN-PUBLICATION DATA
Van Zee, Amy.
  Michigan / by Amy Van Zee.
     p. cm.
  Includes bibliographical references and index.
  ISBN 978-1-60253-466-7 (library bound : alk. paper)
  1. Michigan—Juvenile literature. I. Title.

F566.3.V36 2010
977.4—dc22

                              2010017718

Printed in the United States of America in Mankato, Minnesota.
July 2010
F11538

On the cover:
People enjoy visiting
Mackinac Island
in Michigan.

CONTENTS

Geography

Let's explore Michigan! Michigan is in the northern United States. It has two land areas. They are called the Upper **Peninsula** and the Lower Peninsula.

A bridge connects the two land areas of Michigan.

MINNESOTA

Lake Superior

ONTARIO CANADA

Sault Sainte Marie

Marquette

Tahquamenon Falls

Mackinac Island

Iron Mountain

Fort Mackinac

Mackinaw City

WISCONSIN

Lake Michigan

• Grayling

Cadillac •

Lake Huron

Mt. Pleasant •

Cass City

MICHIGAN

ONTARIO CANADA

NORTH
WEST EAST
SOUTH

Windmill Island Park

Grand Rapids •

Flint •

Holland •

Lansing ★

Ann Arbor •

Kalamazoo •

Detroit •

IOWA

ILLINOIS

Eau Claire •

Detroit River

Lake Erie

INDIANA

OHIO

5

Cities

Lansing is the capital of Michigan. Detroit is the largest city. Grand Rapids, Ann Arbor, and Flint are large cities in the Lower Peninsula. Marquette is a large city in the Upper Peninsula.

Many buildings in downtown Detroit overlook the Detroit River. ▶

Land

Four of the five Great Lakes border Michigan: Lake Erie, Lake Huron, Lake Michigan, and Lake Superior. Michigan has hills, **swamps**, and forests. Waterfalls, rivers, islands, and lakes are found in Michigan, too.

Michigan has about 3,300 miles (5,311 km) of shoreline.

This waterfall, which is part of Tahquamenon Falls in Michigan, drops about 50 feet (15.2 m). ▶

Plants and Animals

Much of Michigan has forests. The white pine is the state tree. Its leaves are sharp like needles. Michigan's state bird is the robin. It is known for its red chest. The bird sings loudly in the spring and summer. The state flower is the apple blossom. It is a pink and white flower.

Apple blossoms open on an apple tree. ▶

People and Work

More than 10 million people live in Michigan. Most of these people live in or near large cities. Many people work in **manufacturing**. They make cars and car parts. Some work in farming or fishing.

Car manufacturing provides many people with jobs in Michigan. ▶

History

Native Americans have lived in the Michigan area for thousands of years. They lived there when the first explorers from Europe came to the area in the 1600s. In the 1700s, England and France fought for the area. But the United States gained the land in 1783. The Michigan area became part of the Northwest **Territory**. Michigan became the twenty-sixth state on January 26, 1837.

The Ottawa is one Native American **tribe** that has lived in Michigan. ▶

Ways of Life

Some people come to Michigan to hunt and fish in the forests and lakes. Skiing is also popular. Other people take part in events that honor Michigan's history of making cars. Music is important in Detroit, too.

Many people in Michigan enjoy fly-fishing. ▶

Famous People

Carmaker Henry Ford was born in Michigan. Movie **director** Francis Ford Coppola was born in Detroit. Singer Diana Ross and basketball player Earvin "Magic" Johnson were also born in Michigan.

Henry Ford started the Ford Motor Company in 1902. ▶

Famous Places

Visitors to Michigan can see the Henry Ford **Museum**. It has pictures and stories that tell the history of making cars. People also like to visit **Windmill** Island Park to see the **Dutch** windmill. Mackinac Island is a popular vacation spot. Fort Mackinac is on the island.

Many visitors see the Dutch windmill during the Tulip Time **Festival** in Holland, Michigan. ▶

The Tulip Time Festival is held each spring when tulips are blooming. The festival celebrates the city's Dutch culture.

21

State Symbols

Seal

Michigan's state seal has the Latin word "Tuebor." It means, "I will defend." Go to **childsworld.com/links** for a link to Michigan's state Web site, where you can get a firsthand look at the state seal.

Flag

The seal is also on the flag. An elk and a moose are on both the seal and the flag.

Quarter

The Michigan state quarter shows the Great Lakes. It came out in 2004.

Glossary

culture (KUL-chur): Culture refers to the art and manners of a group of people. The Tulip Time Festival celebrates Dutch culture.

director (duh-REK-tur): A director is a person in charge of making a movie. Francis Ford Coppola is a director from Michigan.

Dutch (DUCH): Dutch means from the Netherlands, a country in Europe. Windmill Island Park has a Dutch windmill.

festival (FESS-tih-vul): A festival is a celebration for an event or holiday. The Tulip Time Festival is held each year in Holland, Michigan.

manufacturing (man-yuh-FAK-chur-ing): Manufacturing is the task of making items with machines. Some people in Michigan work in manufacturing.

museum (myoo-ZEE-um): A museum is a place where people go to see art, history, or science displays. The Henry Ford Museum is in Michigan.

peninsula (puh-NIN-suh-luh): A peninsula is an area of land that sticks out from the main part of the land and into water. Michigan includes the Upper Peninsula and the Lower Peninsula.

seal (SEEL): A seal is a symbol a state uses for government business. A Latin word is on the Michigan seal.

swamps (SWAHMPS): Swamps are areas of land that have plants and are covered in water. Michigan has some swamps.

symbols (SIM-bulz): Symbols are pictures or things that stand for something else. The seal and the flag are Michigan's symbols.

territory (TAYR-uh-tor-ee): A territory is a piece of land that is controlled by another country. Michigan became a part of the Northwest Territory.

tribe (TRYB): A tribe is a group of people who share ancestors and customs. The Ottawa is a Native American tribe that has lived in Michigan.

windmill (WIHND-mil): A windmill is a machine that uses the wind to make power. Windmill Island Park has a Dutch windmill on it.

Further Information

Books

Mader, Jan. *Michigan*. New York: Children's Press, 2003.

McAuliffe, Emily. *Michigan Facts and Symbols*. New York: Hilltop Books, 2003.

Wargin, Kathy-jo, and Ed Wargin. *Look and See Michigan With Me*. Chelsea, MI: Sleeping Bear Press, 2007.

Web Sites

Visit our Web site for links about Michigan: *childsworld.com/links*

Note to Parents, Teachers, and Librarians: We routinely verify our Web links to make sure they are safe and active sites. So encourage your readers to check them out!

Index